Dinosaur Digs

Discovering Velociraptor

Written by Rena Korb
Illustrated by Ted Dawson

Content Consultant:
Kenneth Carpenter
Curator of Lower Vertebrate Paleontology & Chief Preparator
Denver Museum of Nature and Science

magic Wagon

visit us at www.abdopublishing.com

Printed in the United States.

Text by Rena Korb
Illustrations by Ted Dawson
Edited by Jill Sherman
Interior layout and design by Emily Love
Cover design by Emily Love

Library of Congress Cataloging-in-Publication Data
Korb, Rena B.
  Discovering Velociraptor / Rena Korb ; illustrated by Ted Dawson ; content consultant, Kenneth Carpenter.
     p. cm. — (Dinosaur digs)
  ISBN 978-1-60270-110-6
  1. Velociraptor—Juvenile literature. I. Dawson, Ted, 1966- ill. II. Title.
QE862.S3K6737 2008
567.912—dc22
                        2007034048

FOSSIL FINDS

Roy Chapman Andrews and his team spent years digging in an area of the Gobi Desert in Mongolia known as the Flaming Cliffs. In 1923, they discovered *Velociraptor* (vuh-LAH-suh-rap-tuhr). On their digs, they made many other valuable discoveries. They unearthed the first fossils for *Oviraptor* and *Protoceratops*. They uncovered many relatives of horned fossils called *Psittacosaurus*. They even found the first nest of fossil dinosaur eggs.

In 1971, a team digging in the Gobi Desert discovered the fossils of two dinosaurs that had died while fighting. A *Velociraptor* had sunk its foot claw into the neck of a *Protoceratops*. The *Protoceratops* then bit and broke the arm of the *Velociraptor*. Both dinosaurs died in the fight and were later buried in a sandstorm. They stayed locked in this deadly fight for millions of years.

In 1990, paleontologists discovered another *Velociraptor* fossil in the Gobi Desert. What made this fossil so special was the animal's skull. It had holes in it that may have come from the bite of another dinosaur—maybe even another *Velociraptor*. The animal may have been killed during a fight between dinosaurs of the same kind!

Hong stared out the truck's side, watching the Gobi Desert pass in front of his eyes. He could hardly believe his good luck.

Hong knew more about dinosaurs than the average nine-year-old. He read about them after school. He drew pictures of what they might have looked like. He collected fossils. And best of all, he got to go on digs with his father!

Hong's father was a paleontologist who studied dinosaurs. Another group of scientists had invited his father to look for fossils in the deserts of Mongolia. The Gobi Desert was home to many dinosaurs from the Late Cretaceous period. The scientists hoped to find the bones of dinosaurs such as *Velociraptor*. They had said Hong could come, too!

On the drive, Hong and his father talked about some early fossil discoveries in Mongolia. The first dinosaur eggs had been found there. So had the first *Oviraptor* and *Velociraptor* fossils.

"Many scientists see similarities between the *Velociraptor* and birds. Can you see why, Hong?" asked his father.

Hong thought a moment. "I'd guess it's because of the shape of its neck. It curves like an S, the same as birds."

"Good thinking!" exclaimed his father. "*Velociraptor* also laid its eggs in nests like birds and had birdlike eyes. Some scientists even think *Velociraptor* had feathers."

Once they arrived at the site, Hong packed his notebooks and prepared his tools. He was ready to find dinosaurs!

The Gobi Desert stretches thousands of miles across Asia. With so much land to cover, some people might think it would be impossible for scientists to find fossils here. It would be especially difficult since the fossils have been hidden undergound for millions of years.

Velociraptor had a large brain compared to the size of its body. Scientists believe it was one of the smartest dinosaurs.

Hong knew that paleontologists do not just dig anywhere. The best places to look are places where fossils had already been found. Paleontologists follow one important rule for finding fossils: Never dig for bones until you can see them.

Each morning, after the sun had risen, they left their tents to search among the rocks. Some people climbed hills and cliffs. Some crossed dry streambeds. They all peered down at the loose gravel at their feet. It would be so easy to walk right by a fossil. After three days, they had not found any fossils.

On the fourth day, Hong set out with his father. Hong's feet were quick and his eyes were bright. Though his shoulders sometimes sagged in the heat, his hopes did not. As the sun started to drop in the sky, Hong's father said it was time to head back.

"Just a little longer," Hong pleaded.

A few minutes later, Hong saw a grayish white object sticking out from the sand. He knew right away that this was no rock.

Velociraptor was a member of the Dromaeosaur family. These dinosaurs ran on two legs, had long fingers that could grab on to things, and had a big claw on each foot.

"Dad! Look!" Hong pointed.

Father and son knelt down. There, poking out of the gravel, was a jawbone with sharp, curving teeth still attached to it.

"You've done it," said Hong's father, patting him on the back. "You've found us a fossil! Now, can you tell me which one it is?"

Hong thought about the dinosaurs that had lived in Mongolia. *Oviraptor* had no teeth. The teeth of *Protoceratops* had a flat surface for crushing plants. The teeth in this jawbone looked way too sharp for a plant-eating dinosaur. These teeth curved backward. Hong knew this could help the dinosaur get a good hold on its prey.

"I know!" cried Hong. "It's *Velociraptor!*"

"That's right," said Hong's father. "Now, let's go find the rest of the team and show off your dino!"

They marked the spot with a pile of rocks and then hurried away.

As they headed back to the camp, Hong remembered what he had learned about the *Velociraptor*. He could almost see the words and pictures flowing across the pages of his books.

VELOCIRAPTOR! The name means "Speedy Thief." They are about six feet (2 m) long. They run fast on two legs, not four.

Hong knew all the facts. But what else could he learn from being this close to the ancient animal?

Velociraptor ran at about 40 miles per hour (64 km/h). It could keep up this fast speed for only a short time—but long enough for the dinosaur to catch up to and attack its prey!

The team started to unearth the dinosaur almost as soon as the sun had risen the next day. The jawbone lay where they had left it. Hong and his father used small brushes to gently clear off the loose sand.

Hong got a closer look at those terrifying teeth. Not only were they sharp, they were serrated, like the edges of a bread knife. These were the teeth of a carnivore. The jagged edges made it easy for the *Velociraptor* to cut through the flesh of its prey.

Velociraptor ate other dinosaurs. It may have hunted in packs. Working together would have allowed a group of *Velociraptor* to capture animals much larger than themselves.

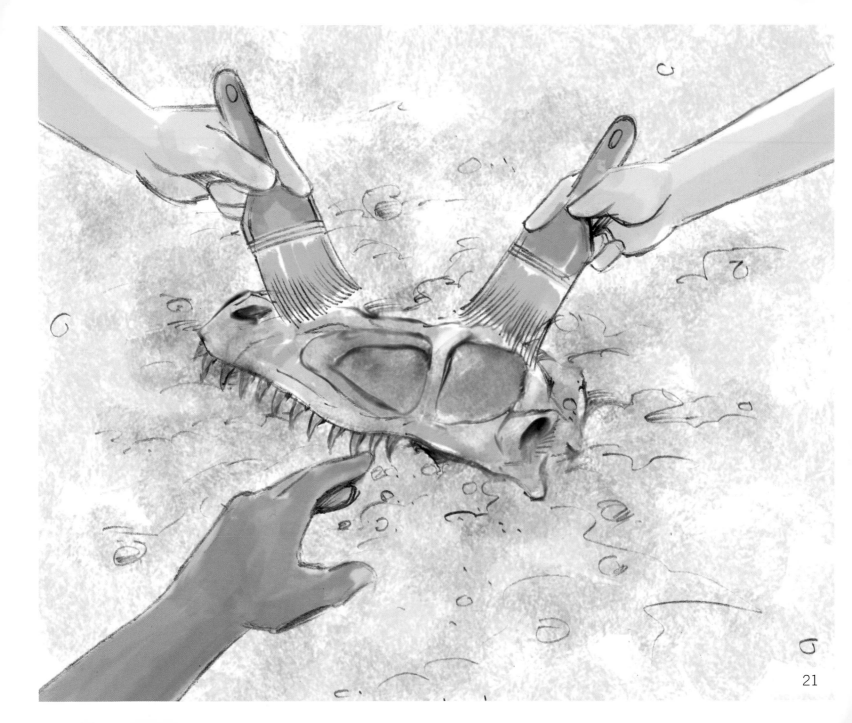

21

The rest of the team had been working to remove the loose gravel and sand from the other bones of the dinosaur. Soon, Hong could see the outline of the animal that had once roamed the land.

Hong pulled out his tape measure. Just like his books said, the animal was about six feet (2 m) long from snout to tail. *Velociraptor* had a long tail that stuck out straight in the air. The tail probably helped *Velociraptor* keep its balance as it swiftly ran and turned. Hong knew that if it had been alive, it would have weighed about 40 pounds (18 kg).

Next, the team took out their awls. These small, sharp tools helped them remove rock that had hardened on the bones. Hong held his breath as they uncovered the feet, and the dinosaur's deadly claws.

Velociraptors had large curved claws on each foot that they used to wound their prey. When it was walking, the dinosaur held the claws off the ground. This kept them very sharp. Now Hong could see for himself why these claws made the animal so frightening.

Once the team had uncovered the entire skeleton, they dug into the ground around it. With small shovels, they cleared as much dirt as possible from beneath the bones. When they were done, the fossil rested on a small island of sandy rock.

The whole team took a moment to look down at their dinosaur. It was now free from its sandy grave. Hong imagined the speedy *Velociraptor* racing across the land, chasing after its dinner.

Velociraptor captured its dinner by using its hands to grab other animals and its claws to wound them. Its prey probably bled to death.

But Hong had only a moment to daydream. They had to get the fossil ready to move. First, they covered the delicate bones with thin, liquid glue to hold them in place. Next, they wrapped a layer of tissue paper around the bones and then used burlap and plaster to wrap them up.

When the skeleton looked like a mummy, their work was done. The *Velociraptor* would be sent home. Hong hoped that the find from this trip would allow scientists to crack more secrets of *Velociraptor!*

Paleontologists spend hundreds of hours removing plaster, sand, and rock from fossils. Only then can they begin to study the bones and figure out their mysteries.

ACTIVITY: Tools for Digging

What does a paleontologist use these tools for?

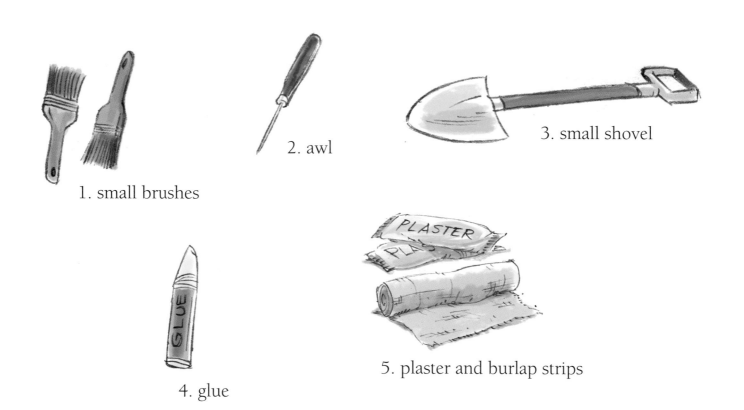

1. small brushes

2. awl

3. small shovel

4. glue

5. plaster and burlap strips

ANSWERS:
1. to remove loose dirt from bones; 2. to scrape away dirt from bones;
3. to clear out dirt around the bones; 4. to hold the bones in place;
5. to wrap up the bones for moving

GLOSSARY

awl — a tool with a sharp point.

carnivore — an animal that eats flesh.

dig — a place where scientists try to recover buried objects by digging.

fossil — the remains of an animal or a plant from a past age, such as a skeleton or a footprint, that has been preserved in the earth or a rock.

paleontologist — (pay-lee-ahn-TAH-luh-jist) a person who studies fossils and ancient animals and plants.

prey — animals hunted or killed by other animals for food.

serrated — with small V-shaped teeth along the edge, like a saw.

READING LIST

Dingus, Lowell, and Mark A. Norell. *Searching for Velociraptor*. New York: HarperCollins, 1996.

Dixon, Dougal. *Dougal Dixon's Amazing Dinosaurs*. Honesdale, PA: Boyds Mill Press, 2000.

Landau, Elaine. *Velociraptor*. New York: Children's Press, 2007.

Marrin, Albert. *Secrets from the Rocks*. New York: Dutton Children's Books, 2002.

ON THE WEB

To learn more about *Velociraptor*, visit ABDO Publishing Company on the World Wide Web at **www.abdopublishing.com**. Web sites about *Velociraptor* are featured on our Book Links page. These links are routinely monitored and updated to provide the most current information available.